50 Classic American Dishes for Home

By: Kelly Johnson

Table of Contents

- Macaroni and Cheese
- Meatloaf
- Chicken Pot Pie
- Beef Stew
- Grilled Cheese Sandwich
- Clam Chowder
- Fried Chicken
- Buffalo Wings
- Sloppy Joes
- Cornbread
- BBQ Ribs
- Shrimp and Grits
- Cheeseburger
- Jambalaya
- Caesar Salad
- Baked Ziti
- Chicken Fried Steak
- New England Boiled Dinner
- Chili
- Philly Cheesesteak
- Pulled Pork Sandwiches
- Hot Dogs
- Corn on the Cob
- Biscuits and Gravy
- Pumpkin Pie
- Apple Pie
- Cobb Salad
- Southern Biscuits
- Beef Tacos
- Chicken Wings
- Grilled Salmon
- Shepherd's Pie
- Meatball Sub
- Roast Turkey with Gravy
- Potato Salad

- Fish Tacos
- BLT Sandwich
- Fried Green Tomatoes
- Spaghetti and Meatballs
- Stuffed Bell Peppers
- Chicken and Waffles
- Fried Catfish
- Shrimp Cocktail
- Nachos
- Grits with Shrimp
- Egg Salad
- Hot Roast Beef Sandwich
- Fried Mozzarella Sticks
- Nachos Supreme
- Rice Pudding

Macaroni and Cheese

Ingredients:

- 8 oz elbow macaroni
- 2 cups shredded cheddar cheese
- 1/2 cup grated Parmesan cheese
- 2 cups milk
- 1/4 cup butter
- 2 tbsp all-purpose flour
- 1/2 tsp garlic powder
- 1/2 tsp mustard powder
- Salt and pepper to taste

Instructions:

1. Cook the macaroni according to the package instructions, then drain and set aside.
2. In a saucepan, melt the butter over medium heat. Add the flour, garlic powder, mustard powder, and cook for 1 minute, whisking constantly.
3. Slowly pour in the milk, whisking continuously until smooth and thickened.
4. Stir in the cheddar and Parmesan cheeses, salt, and pepper, and cook until melted and smooth.
5. Combine the cooked macaroni with the cheese sauce and stir until well coated.
6. Serve hot.

Meatloaf

Ingredients:

- 1 lb ground beef
- 1/2 cup breadcrumbs
- 1/4 cup milk
- 1/4 cup ketchup
- 1/2 onion, finely chopped
- 1 egg
- 1 tsp garlic powder
- 1 tsp dried oregano
- Salt and pepper to taste
- 1/4 cup ketchup (for topping)

Instructions:

1. Preheat the oven to 375°F (190°C).
2. In a bowl, combine ground beef, breadcrumbs, milk, ketchup, onion, egg, garlic powder, oregano, salt, and pepper. Mix well.
3. Form the mixture into a loaf and place it in a greased loaf pan.
4. Spread ketchup on top of the meatloaf.
5. Bake for 45-55 minutes until cooked through and golden on top.
6. Let rest for 10 minutes before slicing and serving.

Chicken Pot Pie

Ingredients:

- 1 lb cooked chicken, diced
- 1 cup frozen peas and carrots
- 1/2 cup butter
- 1/2 cup all-purpose flour
- 2 cups chicken broth
- 1 cup milk
- 1 tsp garlic powder
- 1 tsp onion powder
- Salt and pepper to taste
- 2 pre-made pie crusts

Instructions:

1. Preheat the oven to 425°F (220°C).
2. In a saucepan, melt the butter over medium heat. Add the flour and whisk for 1 minute.
3. Gradually add the chicken broth and milk, stirring constantly until the mixture thickens.
4. Stir in the garlic powder, onion powder, salt, pepper, cooked chicken, and frozen peas and carrots. Mix well.
5. Place one pie crust in the bottom of a pie dish. Pour the chicken mixture into the crust.
6. Top with the second pie crust, sealing the edges. Cut a few slits in the top to allow steam to escape.
7. Bake for 30-35 minutes, until golden brown. Let cool for 10 minutes before serving.

Beef Stew

Ingredients:

- 1 lb beef stew meat, cubed
- 1 tbsp olive oil
- 1 onion, chopped
- 2 garlic cloves, minced
- 2 cups beef broth
- 2 cups water
- 4 carrots, sliced
- 3 potatoes, diced
- 2 celery stalks, chopped
- 1 bay leaf
- 1 tsp thyme
- Salt and pepper to taste

Instructions:

1. In a large pot, heat olive oil over medium heat. Add the beef and brown on all sides. Remove from the pot and set aside.
2. Add the onion and garlic to the pot, cooking until softened, about 3-4 minutes.
3. Return the beef to the pot and add beef broth, water, carrots, potatoes, celery, bay leaf, thyme, salt, and pepper.
4. Bring to a boil, then reduce the heat to low and simmer for 1.5 to 2 hours, until the beef is tender.
5. Remove the bay leaf before serving.

Grilled Cheese Sandwich

Ingredients:

- 2 slices bread
- 2 tbsp butter
- 2 slices cheese (cheddar, American, or your preference)

Instructions:

1. Heat a skillet over medium heat.
2. Butter one side of each slice of bread.
3. Place one slice of bread, butter-side down, onto the skillet. Top with cheese slices and the second slice of bread, butter-side up.
4. Grill the sandwich until golden brown and the cheese is melted, about 3-4 minutes per side.
5. Slice and serve hot.

Clam Chowder

Ingredients:

- 2 cans (6.5 oz each) chopped clams, drained
- 1/2 cup bacon, chopped
- 1 onion, chopped
- 2 cups potatoes, diced
- 1 1/2 cups chicken broth
- 1 1/2 cups heavy cream
- 1/4 cup butter
- 1 tsp thyme
- Salt and pepper to taste

Instructions:

1. In a large pot, cook the bacon over medium heat until crispy. Remove and set aside.
2. In the same pot, add onion and cook until softened, about 3-4 minutes.
3. Add the potatoes, chicken broth, and thyme. Bring to a boil, then reduce the heat and simmer for 15 minutes until the potatoes are tender.
4. Stir in the clams, heavy cream, butter, salt, and pepper. Cook for 5 minutes until heated through.
5. Top with crispy bacon and serve.

Fried Chicken

Ingredients:

- 4 chicken pieces (legs, thighs, or breasts)
- 1 cup buttermilk
- 1 tsp paprika
- 1 tsp garlic powder
- 1 tsp salt
- 1/2 tsp pepper
- 1 cup all-purpose flour
- Vegetable oil for frying

Instructions:

1. Marinate the chicken in buttermilk, paprika, garlic powder, salt, and pepper for at least 1 hour.
2. In a bowl, combine flour with a pinch of salt and pepper.
3. Heat vegetable oil in a large skillet over medium-high heat.
4. Dredge the marinated chicken in the flour mixture, coating it evenly.
5. Fry the chicken for 8-10 minutes per side, or until golden brown and cooked through.
6. Drain on paper towels before serving.

Buffalo Wings

Ingredients:

- 12 chicken wings, split into drumettes and flats
- 1/2 cup hot sauce
- 1/4 cup unsalted butter, melted
- 1 tbsp white vinegar
- 1 tsp garlic powder
- 1/2 tsp paprika
- Salt and pepper to taste

Instructions:

1. Preheat the oven to 400°F (200°C). Line a baking sheet with parchment paper.
2. Arrange the wings in a single layer on the baking sheet. Season with salt and pepper.
3. Bake for 25-30 minutes, turning halfway, until crispy and cooked through.
4. In a bowl, mix together the hot sauce, butter, vinegar, garlic powder, and paprika.
5. Toss the cooked wings in the buffalo sauce mixture until coated.
6. Serve with celery and blue cheese dressing.

Sloppy Joes

Ingredients:

- 1 lb ground beef
- 1 small onion, chopped
- 1 green bell pepper, chopped
- 1 cup ketchup
- 2 tbsp Worcestershire sauce
- 2 tbsp brown sugar
- 1 tbsp Dijon mustard
- 1 tbsp vinegar
- Salt and pepper to taste
- 4 hamburger buns

Instructions:

1. In a skillet, brown the ground beef over medium heat. Drain excess fat.
2. Add the chopped onion and bell pepper, and cook for 3-4 minutes until softened.
3. Stir in ketchup, Worcestershire sauce, brown sugar, Dijon mustard, vinegar, salt, and pepper.
4. Simmer for 10-15 minutes, stirring occasionally, until the mixture thickens.
5. Serve the sloppy joe mixture on toasted hamburger buns.

Cornbread

Ingredients:

- 1 cup cornmeal
- 1 cup all-purpose flour
- 1/4 cup sugar
- 1 tbsp baking powder
- 1/2 tsp salt
- 1 cup milk
- 2 eggs
- 1/4 cup melted butter

Instructions:

1. Preheat the oven to 400°F (200°C). Grease a 9-inch square baking pan.
2. In a bowl, combine cornmeal, flour, sugar, baking powder, and salt.
3. In a separate bowl, whisk together milk, eggs, and melted butter.
4. Pour the wet ingredients into the dry ingredients and stir until just combined.
5. Pour the batter into the prepared pan and bake for 20-25 minutes, until golden brown.
6. Let cool for a few minutes before serving.

BBQ Ribs

Ingredients:

- 2 racks baby back ribs
- 1/4 cup brown sugar
- 1/4 cup paprika
- 1 tbsp garlic powder
- 1 tbsp onion powder
- 1 tbsp chili powder
- 1 tsp cumin
- Salt and pepper to taste
- 2 cups BBQ sauce

Instructions:

1. Preheat the oven to 275°F (135°C). Line a baking sheet with aluminum foil.
2. Remove the membrane from the back of the ribs and pat them dry.
3. Mix brown sugar, paprika, garlic powder, onion powder, chili powder, cumin, salt, and pepper.
4. Rub the spice mixture all over the ribs.
5. Place the ribs on the baking sheet and cover with foil. Bake for 2.5 to 3 hours.
6. Preheat the grill to medium-high heat. Grill the ribs for 5-10 minutes, brushing with BBQ sauce.
7. Slice and serve.

Shrimp and Grits

Ingredients:

- 1 lb shrimp, peeled and deveined
- 1 cup grits
- 4 cups water
- 2 tbsp butter
- 1/2 cup heavy cream
- 2 cloves garlic, minced
- 1/4 tsp paprika
- Salt and pepper to taste
- 2 tbsp chopped parsley

Instructions:

1. Cook the grits according to package instructions, adding water, butter, and heavy cream. Stir in salt and pepper.
2. In a skillet, sauté garlic in butter over medium heat for 1-2 minutes.
3. Add the shrimp, paprika, salt, and pepper. Cook for 3-4 minutes until the shrimp are pink and cooked through.
4. Serve the shrimp over the creamy grits and garnish with parsley.

Cheeseburger

Ingredients:

- 1 lb ground beef
- Salt and pepper to taste
- 4 hamburger buns
- 4 slices cheddar cheese
- Lettuce, tomato, onion (optional)
- Ketchup and mustard (optional)

Instructions:

1. Form the ground beef into 4 patties. Season with salt and pepper.
2. Heat a grill or skillet over medium-high heat. Cook the patties for 3-4 minutes per side.
3. Add a slice of cheese to each patty in the last minute of cooking.
4. Toast the buns on the grill or in a skillet.
5. Assemble the burgers with lettuce, tomato, onion, ketchup, and mustard, if desired.

Jambalaya

Ingredients:

- 1 lb chicken breast, diced
- 1/2 lb sausage, sliced
- 1 onion, chopped
- 1 bell pepper, chopped
- 2 cloves garlic, minced
- 1 can diced tomatoes
- 1 1/2 cups rice
- 3 cups chicken broth
- 1 tsp paprika
- 1 tsp thyme
- 1/2 tsp cayenne pepper
- Salt and pepper to taste

Instructions:

1. In a large pot, brown the chicken and sausage over medium heat. Remove and set aside.
2. In the same pot, sauté onion, bell pepper, and garlic until softened.
3. Stir in diced tomatoes, rice, chicken broth, paprika, thyme, cayenne pepper, salt, and pepper.
4. Return the chicken and sausage to the pot. Bring to a boil, then reduce heat and simmer for 20-25 minutes, until the rice is cooked and liquid is absorbed.
5. Serve hot.

Caesar Salad

Ingredients:

- 1 head Romaine lettuce, chopped
- 1/4 cup Caesar dressing
- 1/4 cup grated Parmesan cheese
- Croutons

Instructions:

1. Toss the chopped lettuce with Caesar dressing until evenly coated.
2. Sprinkle with Parmesan cheese and top with croutons.
3. Serve immediately.

Baked Ziti

Ingredients:

- 1 lb ziti pasta
- 2 cups marinara sauce
- 2 cups ricotta cheese
- 2 cups shredded mozzarella cheese
- 1/2 cup grated Parmesan cheese
- 1 egg
- 1 tbsp chopped basil

Instructions:

1. Preheat the oven to 375°F (190°C). Cook the ziti according to package instructions and drain.
2. In a bowl, mix ricotta cheese, 1 cup of mozzarella, Parmesan cheese, egg, and basil.
3. In a baking dish, layer the cooked ziti, ricotta mixture, and marinara sauce.
4. Top with the remaining mozzarella and bake for 25-30 minutes, until bubbly and golden.
5. Let cool for a few minutes before serving.

Chicken Fried Steak

Ingredients:

- 4 beef steaks (cube steaks or round steaks)
- 1 cup flour
- 1 tsp garlic powder
- 1 tsp paprika
- Salt and pepper to taste
- 2 eggs, beaten
- 1 cup buttermilk
- Vegetable oil for frying

Instructions:

1. In a bowl, combine flour, garlic powder, paprika, salt, and pepper.
2. Dip each steak into the egg, then dredge in the flour mixture.
3. Heat oil in a skillet over medium-high heat. Fry the steaks for 3-4 minutes per side, until golden and crispy.
4. Drain on paper towels and serve with gravy if desired.

New England Boiled Dinner

Ingredients:

- 1 lb corned beef
- 4 large potatoes, peeled and quartered
- 4 carrots, peeled and cut into chunks
- 1 onion, quartered
- 1/2 head cabbage, cut into wedges
- Salt and pepper to taste

Instructions:

1. In a large pot, place the corned beef and cover with water. Bring to a boil, then simmer for 2-3 hours until the meat is tender.
2. Add potatoes, carrots, and onion to the pot. Simmer for an additional 30 minutes.
3. Add the cabbage and cook for another 10-15 minutes until tender.
4. Remove the meat and slice. Serve with the vegetables.

Chili

Ingredients:

- 1 lb ground beef or turkey
- 1 onion, chopped
- 1 bell pepper, chopped
- 2 cloves garlic, minced
- 1 can diced tomatoes
- 1 can kidney beans, drained and rinsed
- 1 can black beans, drained and rinsed
- 1 tbsp chili powder
- 1 tsp cumin
- 1 tsp paprika
- Salt and pepper to taste
- 1/4 cup tomato paste
- 1 cup beef or vegetable broth

Instructions:

1. In a large pot, brown the ground meat over medium heat. Drain excess fat.
2. Add the onion, bell pepper, and garlic. Cook until softened.
3. Stir in diced tomatoes, beans, chili powder, cumin, paprika, salt, pepper, tomato paste, and broth.
4. Bring to a boil, then reduce heat and simmer for 30-40 minutes.
5. Serve hot with shredded cheese, sour cream, and cornbread if desired.

Philly Cheesesteak

Ingredients:

- 1 lb ribeye steak, thinly sliced
- 1 onion, thinly sliced
- 1 bell pepper, thinly sliced (optional)
- 4 hoagie rolls
- 4 slices provolone or American cheese
- 2 tbsp vegetable oil
- Salt and pepper to taste

Instructions:

1. Heat oil in a skillet over medium heat. Add onion (and bell pepper if using) and sauté until softened, about 5-7 minutes.
2. In the same skillet, add the thinly sliced steak and cook until browned, 5-6 minutes. Season with salt and pepper.
3. Divide the steak mixture between the hoagie rolls and top each with a slice of cheese.
4. Serve immediately, optionally adding sautéed mushrooms or hot sauce.

Pulled Pork Sandwiches

Ingredients:

- 2 lb pork shoulder
- 1 onion, chopped
- 2 cloves garlic, minced
- 1 cup BBQ sauce
- 1 tbsp apple cider vinegar
- 1 tbsp brown sugar
- Salt and pepper to taste
- 4 hamburger buns

Instructions:

1. Season the pork shoulder with salt and pepper. Place it in a slow cooker with the onion and garlic.
2. In a bowl, mix BBQ sauce, vinegar, and brown sugar. Pour over the pork.
3. Cover and cook on low for 6-8 hours or until the pork is tender and can be easily shredded.
4. Shred the pork with a fork and mix it with the sauce.
5. Serve on buns with extra BBQ sauce if desired.

Hot Dogs

Ingredients:

- 4 hot dog sausages
- 4 hot dog buns
- Mustard, ketchup, onions, relish, and any other desired toppings

Instructions:

1. Grill or boil the hot dog sausages until heated through.
2. Place each sausage in a bun.
3. Add your preferred toppings, such as mustard, ketchup, onions, or relish.

Corn on the Cob

Ingredients:

- 4 ears of corn, husked
- Salt to taste
- Butter (optional)

Instructions:

1. Bring a large pot of water to a boil. Add the corn and cook for 7-10 minutes, or until tender.
2. Remove the corn from the water and season with salt.
3. Optionally, serve with butter.

Biscuits and Gravy

Ingredients for Biscuits:

- 2 cups all-purpose flour
- 2 tsp baking powder
- 1/2 tsp salt
- 1/2 cup cold butter
- 3/4 cup milk

Ingredients for Gravy:

- 1/2 lb sausage, crumbled
- 2 tbsp flour
- 2 cups milk
- Salt and pepper to taste

Instructions:

1. Preheat the oven to 450°F (230°C).
2. In a bowl, mix the flour, baking powder, and salt. Cut in the cold butter until the mixture resembles coarse crumbs.
3. Stir in the milk to form a dough. Pat the dough into a 1-inch thick circle and cut into biscuits.
4. Bake the biscuits for 10-12 minutes until golden brown.
5. For the gravy, cook the sausage in a skillet over medium heat until browned. Sprinkle in the flour and cook for 1-2 minutes.
6. Slowly add the milk, stirring constantly until the gravy thickens. Season with salt and pepper.
7. Serve the biscuits with the gravy poured over them.

Pumpkin Pie

Ingredients:

- 1 (15 oz) can pumpkin puree
- 1 cup heavy cream
- 3/4 cup brown sugar
- 2 eggs
- 1 tsp cinnamon
- 1/2 tsp nutmeg
- 1/4 tsp ginger
- 1/4 tsp salt
- 1 pie crust (store-bought or homemade)

Instructions:

1. Preheat the oven to 425°F (220°C).
2. In a bowl, whisk together pumpkin puree, heavy cream, brown sugar, eggs, cinnamon, nutmeg, ginger, and salt until smooth.
3. Pour the filling into the pie crust.
4. Bake for 15 minutes, then reduce the temperature to 350°F (175°C) and bake for 45-50 minutes, until the center is set.
5. Let the pie cool before serving.

Apple Pie

Ingredients:

- 6 cups apples, peeled, cored, and sliced
- 3/4 cup sugar
- 2 tbsp flour
- 1 tsp cinnamon
- 1/4 tsp nutmeg
- 1 tbsp lemon juice
- 1 tbsp butter, diced
- 1 pie crust (store-bought or homemade)

Instructions:

1. Preheat the oven to 425°F (220°C).
2. In a bowl, combine apples, sugar, flour, cinnamon, nutmeg, and lemon juice.
3. Roll out the pie crust and place it in a pie dish. Fill with the apple mixture.
4. Dot the apples with butter and top with the second pie crust. Crimp the edges and cut a few slits in the top for steam to escape.
5. Bake for 40-45 minutes, until the crust is golden and the filling is bubbly.
6. Let the pie cool before serving.

Cobb Salad

Ingredients:

- 4 cups mixed greens
- 2 hard-boiled eggs, sliced
- 1 cup cooked chicken breast, chopped
- 1 avocado, diced
- 1 cup cherry tomatoes, halved
- 1/2 cup crumbled blue cheese
- 1/2 cup cooked bacon, crumbled
- 1/4 cup red onion, thinly sliced
- 1/4 cup ranch or blue cheese dressing

Instructions:

1. In a large salad bowl, layer the mixed greens, followed by rows of eggs, chicken, avocado, tomatoes, blue cheese, bacon, and red onion.
2. Drizzle with ranch or blue cheese dressing.
3. Serve immediately.

Southern Biscuits

Ingredients:

- 2 cups all-purpose flour
- 2 tsp baking powder
- 1/2 tsp salt
- 1/2 cup cold butter, cubed
- 3/4 cup buttermilk

Instructions:

1. Preheat the oven to 450°F (230°C).
2. In a large bowl, mix the flour, baking powder, and salt.
3. Cut in the cold butter until the mixture resembles coarse crumbs.
4. Stir in the buttermilk to form a dough. Be careful not to overwork it.
5. Turn the dough out onto a floured surface and gently pat it into a 1-inch thick rectangle.
6. Use a biscuit cutter to cut out biscuits and place them on a baking sheet.
7. Bake for 10-12 minutes or until golden brown.
8. Serve with butter, jam, or gravy.

Beef Tacos

Ingredients:

- 1 lb ground beef
- 1 onion, chopped
- 1 packet taco seasoning or 1 tbsp homemade seasoning
- 1/2 cup water
- 8 taco shells
- Lettuce, shredded
- Tomato, diced
- Shredded cheese
- Sour cream

Instructions:

1. Brown the ground beef with the chopped onion in a skillet over medium heat. Drain any excess fat.
2. Stir in the taco seasoning and water, simmer for 5-7 minutes.
3. Warm the taco shells according to the package instructions.
4. Fill each shell with the beef mixture and top with lettuce, tomato, cheese, and sour cream.
5. Serve immediately.

Chicken Wings

Ingredients:

- 2 lbs chicken wings
- 1/4 cup olive oil
- 1 tbsp garlic powder
- 1 tsp paprika
- Salt and pepper to taste
- 1/4 cup hot sauce (optional)
- Blue cheese or ranch dressing for dipping

Instructions:

1. Preheat the oven to 400°F (200°C).
2. Toss the chicken wings with olive oil, garlic powder, paprika, salt, and pepper.
3. Spread the wings in a single layer on a baking sheet.
4. Bake for 25-30 minutes or until crispy and golden brown.
5. If using hot sauce, toss the wings in the sauce after baking.
6. Serve with blue cheese or ranch dressing.

Grilled Salmon

Ingredients:

- 4 salmon fillets
- 2 tbsp olive oil
- 1 tbsp lemon juice
- Salt and pepper to taste
- Fresh herbs (optional)

Instructions:

1. Preheat the grill to medium-high heat.
2. Brush the salmon fillets with olive oil and lemon juice, then season with salt and pepper.
3. Grill the salmon for 4-5 minutes per side, or until the salmon easily flakes with a fork.
4. Garnish with fresh herbs and serve.

Shepherd's Pie

Ingredients:

- 1 lb ground lamb or beef
- 1 onion, chopped
- 2 carrots, diced
- 2 cloves garlic, minced
- 1 cup frozen peas
- 2 tbsp tomato paste
- 1 cup beef broth
- 2 cups mashed potatoes
- 1 tbsp olive oil
- Salt and pepper to taste

Instructions:

1. Preheat the oven to 375°F (190°C).
2. In a skillet, heat olive oil and cook the ground meat until browned.
3. Add the onion, carrots, and garlic. Cook for 5 minutes until softened.
4. Stir in the tomato paste, beef broth, and peas. Simmer for 10 minutes.
5. Season with salt and pepper to taste.
6. Transfer the meat mixture to a baking dish, then spread mashed potatoes over the top.
7. Bake for 20-25 minutes, or until the top is golden.
8. Serve hot.

Meatball Sub

Ingredients:

- 1 lb ground beef or pork
- 1/4 cup breadcrumbs
- 1 egg
- 1/4 cup Parmesan cheese
- 1 tsp garlic powder
- 1 cup marinara sauce
- 4 hoagie rolls
- 1 cup shredded mozzarella cheese

Instructions:

1. Preheat the oven to 375°F (190°C).
2. In a bowl, combine the ground meat, breadcrumbs, egg, Parmesan, garlic powder, salt, and pepper. Form into meatballs.
3. Brown the meatballs in a skillet, then add marinara sauce. Simmer for 10 minutes.
4. Split the hoagie rolls and place meatballs in each.
5. Top with marinara sauce and shredded mozzarella.
6. Bake for 10 minutes, until the cheese is melted and bubbly.
7. Serve immediately.

Roast Turkey with Gravy

Ingredients for Turkey:

- 1 whole turkey (12-14 lbs)
- 1/4 cup olive oil
- Salt and pepper
- Fresh herbs (thyme, rosemary, sage)

Ingredients for Gravy:

- 1/4 cup turkey drippings
- 1/4 cup flour
- 2 cups turkey broth

Instructions for Turkey:

1. Preheat the oven to 325°F (165°C).
2. Rub the turkey with olive oil and season generously with salt, pepper, and fresh herbs.
3. Roast the turkey for about 3-4 hours, or until the internal temperature reaches 165°F (75°C).
4. Let the turkey rest for 20 minutes before carving.

Instructions for Gravy:

1. In a saucepan, heat the turkey drippings and whisk in the flour.
2. Gradually add turkey broth, stirring constantly. Simmer until thickened.
3. Season with salt and pepper.

Potato Salad

Ingredients:

- 4 cups boiled potatoes, diced
- 1/2 cup mayonnaise
- 1 tbsp Dijon mustard
- 1/4 cup chopped celery
- 1/4 cup chopped onion
- Salt and pepper to taste
- 2 hard-boiled eggs, chopped

Instructions:

1. In a large bowl, combine the potatoes, mayonnaise, mustard, celery, onion, and hard-boiled eggs.
2. Season with salt and pepper to taste.
3. Chill for at least 1 hour before serving.

Fish Tacos

Ingredients:

- 1 lb white fish fillets (tilapia, cod, or mahi-mahi)
- 1 tbsp olive oil
- 1 tsp chili powder
- 1 tsp cumin
- 8 small tortillas
- Shredded cabbage
- Salsa
- Lime wedges
- Sour cream or crema

Instructions:

1. Preheat the grill or a skillet over medium-high heat.
2. Rub the fish fillets with olive oil and season with chili powder, cumin, salt, and pepper.
3. Grill the fish for 3-4 minutes per side, or until cooked through.
4. Warm the tortillas, then assemble the tacos with fish, shredded cabbage, salsa, and a dollop of sour cream.
5. Serve with lime wedges.

BLT Sandwich

Ingredients:

- 4 slices bacon
- 2 slices bread (toasted)
- Lettuce leaves
- Tomato slices
- Mayonnaise

Instructions:

1. Cook the bacon in a skillet until crispy, then drain on paper towels.
2. Spread mayonnaise on each slice of toast.
3. Layer the bacon, lettuce, and tomato slices on one piece of toast, then top with the other.
4. Serve immediately.

Fried Green Tomatoes

Ingredients:

- 4-5 green tomatoes, sliced 1/4 inch thick
- 1 cup cornmeal
- 1/2 cup all-purpose flour
- 1 tsp salt
- 1/2 tsp black pepper
- 1/2 tsp paprika
- 2 eggs
- 1/4 cup buttermilk
- Vegetable oil for frying

Instructions:

1. In a shallow dish, combine the cornmeal, flour, salt, pepper, and paprika.
2. In another dish, whisk together the eggs and buttermilk.
3. Dip each tomato slice into the egg mixture, then coat it in the cornmeal mixture.
4. Heat vegetable oil in a skillet over medium heat.
5. Fry the tomato slices in batches for about 3 minutes per side, or until golden brown.
6. Drain on paper towels and serve with your favorite dipping sauce.

Spaghetti and Meatballs

Ingredients for Meatballs:

- 1 lb ground beef
- 1/4 cup breadcrumbs
- 1/4 cup grated Parmesan cheese
- 1/4 cup chopped parsley
- 1 egg
- 2 cloves garlic, minced
- Salt and pepper to taste

Ingredients for Sauce:

- 2 cups marinara sauce
- 1 tbsp olive oil
- 1 tsp garlic powder
- 1 tsp dried basil
- 1/2 tsp dried oregano

For Spaghetti:

- 1 lb spaghetti
- Salt for boiling

Instructions:

1. Preheat the oven to 375°F (190°C).
2. In a bowl, mix together the ground beef, breadcrumbs, Parmesan, parsley, egg, garlic, salt, and pepper. Shape into meatballs.
3. Place the meatballs on a baking sheet and bake for 20-25 minutes, until cooked through.
4. While the meatballs bake, prepare the sauce. In a saucepan, heat olive oil, and add garlic powder, basil, and oregano. Stir in marinara sauce and simmer on low heat.
5. Cook the spaghetti according to package instructions. Drain and set aside.
6. Combine the meatballs with the sauce and simmer for an additional 10 minutes.
7. Serve the meatballs and sauce over spaghetti.

Stuffed Bell Peppers

Ingredients:

- 4 large bell peppers, tops cut off and seeds removed
- 1 lb ground beef or turkey
- 1/2 cup cooked rice
- 1 can (14 oz) diced tomatoes
- 1 onion, chopped
- 2 cloves garlic, minced
- 1 tsp dried oregano
- 1 tsp salt
- 1/2 tsp black pepper
- 1 cup shredded cheese (cheddar, mozzarella, or your choice)

Instructions:

1. Preheat the oven to 375°F (190°C).
2. In a skillet, cook the ground beef (or turkey) with onion and garlic until browned. Drain any excess fat.
3. Stir in the cooked rice, diced tomatoes, oregano, salt, and pepper.
4. Stuff the bell peppers with the meat mixture and place them in a baking dish.
5. Top each stuffed pepper with shredded cheese.
6. Cover the dish with foil and bake for 30 minutes. Uncover and bake for an additional 10 minutes, until the cheese is bubbly.
7. Serve hot.

Chicken and Waffles

Ingredients:

- 4 boneless, skinless chicken breasts
- 1 cup buttermilk
- 1 cup flour
- 1 tsp salt
- 1/2 tsp black pepper
- 1/2 tsp paprika
- Vegetable oil for frying
- 4 waffles (store-bought or homemade)
- Maple syrup for serving

Instructions:

1. In a bowl, soak the chicken breasts in buttermilk for at least 30 minutes.
2. In another bowl, combine the flour, salt, pepper, and paprika.
3. Heat vegetable oil in a skillet over medium-high heat.
4. Dredge the chicken breasts in the seasoned flour mixture, coating them thoroughly.
5. Fry the chicken for 5-7 minutes per side, or until golden and cooked through.
6. Serve the chicken on top of the waffles and drizzle with maple syrup.

Fried Catfish

Ingredients:

- 4 catfish fillets
- 1 cup cornmeal
- 1/2 cup all-purpose flour
- 1 tsp salt
- 1/2 tsp black pepper
- 1 tsp paprika
- 1/2 tsp garlic powder
- 1/4 tsp cayenne pepper (optional)
- 1 egg, beaten
- 1/2 cup buttermilk
- Vegetable oil for frying

Instructions:

1. In a shallow dish, combine the cornmeal, flour, salt, pepper, paprika, garlic powder, and cayenne.
2. In another dish, whisk together the egg and buttermilk.
3. Dip the catfish fillets in the egg mixture, then coat them with the cornmeal mixture.
4. Heat vegetable oil in a skillet over medium heat.
5. Fry the catfish fillets for 4-5 minutes per side, or until crispy and golden brown.
6. Drain on paper towels and serve with tartar sauce or lemon wedges.

Shrimp Cocktail

Ingredients:

- 1 lb large shrimp, peeled and deveined
- 1 lemon, halved
- 2 cloves garlic, smashed
- 1 bay leaf
- 4 cups water
- Salt for seasoning

For Cocktail Sauce:

- 1/2 cup ketchup
- 1 tbsp horseradish
- 1 tbsp lemon juice
- 1 tsp Worcestershire sauce
- A dash of hot sauce (optional)

Instructions:

1. In a large pot, bring water, lemon halves, garlic, bay leaf, and a pinch of salt to a boil.
2. Add the shrimp and cook for 2-3 minutes, until pink and opaque.
3. Remove the shrimp from the pot and chill them in ice water to stop the cooking process.
4. In a small bowl, combine all the cocktail sauce ingredients and mix well.
5. Serve the chilled shrimp with cocktail sauce for dipping.

Nachos

Ingredients:

- 1 bag tortilla chips
- 1 1/2 cups shredded cheddar cheese
- 1 cup diced tomatoes
- 1/2 cup chopped green onions
- 1/2 cup sliced jalapeños
- 1/2 cup sour cream
- 1/4 cup salsa
- 1/4 cup guacamole

Instructions:

1. Preheat the oven to 375°F (190°C).
2. Spread the tortilla chips evenly on a baking sheet.
3. Sprinkle shredded cheese over the chips and add diced tomatoes, green onions, and jalapeños.
4. Bake in the oven for 10-12 minutes, or until the cheese has melted.
5. Serve with sour cream, salsa, and guacamole on the side.

Grits with Shrimp

Ingredients:

- 1 cup grits
- 4 cups water
- 1 lb shrimp, peeled and deveined
- 2 tbsp butter
- 2 cloves garlic, minced
- 1/2 tsp paprika
- Salt and pepper to taste
- 1/2 cup heavy cream
- 1 tbsp fresh parsley, chopped

Instructions:

1. Cook the grits according to package instructions, using 4 cups of water. Stir in butter and season with salt and pepper.
2. In a skillet, melt butter and sauté garlic for 1 minute.
3. Add shrimp, paprika, salt, and pepper, cooking for 2-3 minutes per side until shrimp are pink and cooked through.
4. Stir in heavy cream and cook for an additional 2 minutes.
5. Serve the shrimp mixture over the grits, topped with fresh parsley.

Egg Salad

Ingredients:

- 6 large eggs
- 1/4 cup mayonnaise
- 1 tbsp Dijon mustard
- 1 tbsp white vinegar
- 1/4 cup chopped celery
- 1/4 cup chopped green onions
- Salt and pepper to taste

Instructions:

1. Boil the eggs in a pot of water for 10-12 minutes until hard boiled. Let them cool, peel, and chop.
2. In a bowl, mix mayonnaise, Dijon mustard, and white vinegar.
3. Stir in the chopped eggs, celery, and green onions. Season with salt and pepper to taste.
4. Serve on bread, crackers, or over lettuce.

Hot Roast Beef Sandwich

Ingredients:

- 4 slices of bread (your choice)
- 1 lb roast beef, thinly sliced
- 1/4 cup beef gravy (homemade or store-bought)
- 1 tbsp butter
- 1/4 cup sliced onions
- 1/4 cup shredded cheese (optional)

Instructions:

1. Heat the gravy in a saucepan over medium heat.
2. In a skillet, melt butter and sauté onions until softened, about 5 minutes.
3. Layer the roast beef on the bread and top with sautéed onions. Pour the hot gravy over the beef.
4. Optionally, sprinkle with cheese and place under a broiler to melt.
5. Serve hot with additional gravy on the side.

Fried Mozzarella Sticks

Ingredients:

- 1 lb mozzarella cheese sticks
- 1 cup all-purpose flour
- 2 eggs, beaten
- 1 1/2 cups breadcrumbs
- 1 tsp garlic powder
- 1 tsp dried oregano
- Salt and pepper to taste
- Vegetable oil for frying
- Marinara sauce for dipping

Instructions:

1. Freeze the mozzarella sticks for 30 minutes to firm them up.
2. Set up a breading station: coat the mozzarella sticks in flour, dip in beaten eggs, then coat in breadcrumbs mixed with garlic powder, oregano, salt, and pepper.
3. Heat vegetable oil in a skillet over medium heat.
4. Fry the mozzarella sticks for 2-3 minutes per side, until golden and crispy.
5. Drain on paper towels and serve with marinara sauce.

Nachos Supreme

Ingredients:

- 1 bag tortilla chips
- 1 lb ground beef or chicken
- 1 packet taco seasoning
- 1 1/2 cups shredded cheddar cheese
- 1/2 cup diced tomatoes
- 1/4 cup black olives, sliced
- 1/2 cup sour cream
- 1/4 cup guacamole
- 1/4 cup chopped green onions
- 1/2 cup salsa

Instructions:

1. Preheat the oven to 375°F (190°C).
2. Cook the ground beef or chicken with taco seasoning according to package instructions.
3. Spread the tortilla chips on a baking sheet and top with seasoned meat and shredded cheese.
4. Bake for 10-12 minutes, or until the cheese has melted.
5. Top with diced tomatoes, black olives, sour cream, guacamole, chopped green onions, and salsa.

Rice Pudding

Ingredients:

- 1 cup Arborio rice or short-grain rice
- 4 cups milk
- 1/2 cup sugar
- 1 tsp vanilla extract
- 1/2 tsp ground cinnamon
- 1/4 tsp ground nutmeg
- A pinch of salt

Instructions:

1. In a medium saucepan, combine the rice, milk, sugar, vanilla extract, cinnamon, nutmeg, and salt.
2. Cook over medium heat, stirring frequently, until the mixture thickens and the rice is tender, about 20-25 minutes.
3. Serve warm or chilled, garnished with extra cinnamon or nutmeg if desired.